ATMOSPHERE
**SHIFT**

# ATMOSPHERE SHIFT

## CREATE AN ENVIRONMENT
## WHERE ANYTHING CAN HAPPEN

### MATTHEW K. THOMPSON

XULON PRESS

Xulon Press
2301 Lucien Way #415
Maitland, FL 32751
407.339.4217
www.xulonpress.com

Unless otherwise indicated, Scripture quotations taken from the Holy Bible, New International Version (NIV). Copyright © 1973, 1978, 1984, 2011 by Biblica, Inc.™. Used by permission. All rights reserved.

Printed in the United States of America.
Edited by Xulon Press.

ISBN-13: 9781545639283

# TABLE OF CONTENTS

# DEDICATION

My Love, My Wife, My Dream, My Queen, "he who finds a wife finds a good thing and obtains Favor from the Lord." Thank you Mona for loving me, believing in me and being My Favor.

You are my everything...

## CHAPTER 1

# KAIROS MOMENTS

*Proverbs 23: 7*
*"As a man thinketh in his heart, so is he."*

How we utilize our very existence, every single action we do or chose not to do, begins and ends with our mindset.

## Kairos

I believe that, as of a few seconds ago, you have entered into a Kairos Moment. You just may not know it yet.

The word kairos is an ancient Greek word meaning the right, critical, or opportune moment. The ancient Greeks had two words to signify time: chronos and kairos. Chronos refers to chronological or sequential time, what we refer to as hours, minutes, seconds, etc. Kairos signifies a moment in a person's life destined for something of high importance to occur. In other words, a time in a person's life meant for something life-changing to occur.

I submit to you that you have been on a collision course with this book since before either of you were created. There was a moment in time, appointed long ago, that has manifested itself, materialized itself, as you read.

Some might think it's logical to think differently. After all, it's much easier to think that there is no way you were meant to read this. We have been trained and ingrained to figure every-thing out, to understand something before we allow ourselves to believe in it.

We live and operate in Chronos time. We set our alarms and calendars to it. We rise and go to bed by it. We schedule our date nights, our family vacations, and our church times to it. As spirit beings within a body that decays and dies, we are ruled by Chronos, so much so that, to think outside of it, outside of our perception of time, the very thought becomes illogical and thus we deem it to not be possible.

Until we remember that God is not subject to the ticking of a man-made clock. He is not subjected to operate under the steady movement of time. He operates in time, out of time, and is time all at the same time.

Understanding that you've stepped into a Kairos Moment happens when you lose the ability of trying to figure every-thing out and just completely and utterly trust in God. This is where God, your anointing, and your obedience collide. This is a moment when Heaven opens to you alone and you are given a moment of clarity. A moment when God pours revelation onto and into you.

I believe that such a time is upon you now. For what purpose? Only God knows. But I know this, God is stirring up the atmosphere around His church. I feel as if the Lord has positioned His church to help others shift and create atmospheres where He can move and do His will.

Not only do I believe in Kairos moments but I also believe in Kairos Relationships. Friendships that have and will be forged with the blessing of God designed to help one or the other through upcoming storms. The relationship David and Jonathan had was definitely one. It didn't make sense for the prince to align himself with the very person anointed to take his kingdom. Yet, long before there was an Israel, Jonathan and David were destined to form a bond. The problem today is that while every believer wants to have a David and Jonathan relationship, no one wants to be Jonathan! If you can become a Jonathan to a man or woman of God, you will become a David to God because you will be after His heart.

There are also Kairos Conversations. Perhaps you've had a few. A prophetic time when someone spoke something into your life that marked you. Many Kairos conversations have been recorded in the Bible for us to learn from. For example, Matthew 16 is a record of Jesus asking his disciples, "Who do men say I am?"

They answered, "Some say your John the Baptist, some Elijah, and others Jeremiah or one of the prophets"

I ask you this... who do you say Jesus is? Who is He to you? Not during Sunday worship when the band is in full swing and the assembled voices are singing as one in euphoric worship. Who is He to you when you're alone? Who is He to you when you've been treated unjustly? Who is He to you when you and your spouse are trying to conceive but you just... can't and the doctors tell you it won't happen?

**Who is He to you when you're alone?**

Is your answer to who He is aligned with your political affiliation? Does your description of Him side with whatever news outlet (CNN, NBC, Fox News) you watch? Is your answer to who He is dependent on your race, gender, or income level?

Simon answered and said, "You are the Christ. Son of the living God."

Jesus jumped up and said, "Blessed are you, Simon Bar-Jonah, for flesh and blood has not revealed this to you, but My Father who is in heaven. And I also say to you that you are Peter, and on this rock I will build My church, and the gates of Hades shall not prevail against it."

So, Jesus tells Simon Bar-Jonah that God revealed to him who he was. That he was the son of the living god. In other words, Jesus tells Simon Bar-Jonah, God has revealed to you that I am Kairos. My life on earth is the moment creation has been waiting for since it began. Long before the fall of Adam, I have been and now I am here.

Then, Jesus prophesied over Simon and changed his name. Simon Bar-Jonah is no longer mentioned, Peter, the rock, emerged from that Kairos moment.

Again, I believe a Kairos Moment is upon you, and I pray you provide the faith required for God to continue to mold you into the type of person that shifts and changes atmospheres for His glory. My spirit rejoices when I think of what version of you can emerge after your encounter with this book.

Kairos Moments are typically not for the person experiencing it. For example, God called Moses although he was afraid to confront the Pharaoh. God asked him what he had in his hands. Moses said, "A staff." God instructed Moses to throw it on the ground and the staff became a serpent. Then God told him to grab it by its tail and when Moses did so, it reverted back to a staff. Then God injected leprosy into one of Moses' hands. Then God healed the leprous hand. That entire encounter was a Kairos Moment, a time when something life-changing happened that was destined by God to happen. My point is this – God put Moses through all of that but he didn't do it for Moses. He did it for the multitude.

What I'm saying to you is that God has a purpose and design for you and that's why you're reading this book right now. However, it's not for you to get credit, glory, or respect. It's for you to be used to shift

**It's for you to be used to shift the atmosphere**

the atmosphere so that you impact the generation of people (multitude) around you.

## A Souvenir

I have experienced plenty of trials. Many of which led me to Kairos Moments. When my wife and I got married, we got busy with trying to raise a family. After a period of time, we realized something was amiss. My wife, Mona, and I made an appointment with our doctor and after many tests, he told us that the issue was that Mona was not producing follicles. *(Women begin puberty with about 400,000 follicles, each with the potential to release an egg cell at ovulation for fertilization. These eggs are developed once every menstrual cycle.)*

"What do you mean she's not producing enough follicles?" In my effort to understand, I needed our doctor to clarify things to me. I needed to know how many more we needed to have a child.

"No, you misunderstand me." He answered. "It's not that she's not producing enough, she's not producing any!"

My wife and I are not people that give up easily. We rejected the report the doctor had given us and increased our efforts on having a baby. We also tried all sorts of natural remedies and medicines that our doctor recommended.

We even ate some foods recommended to us from those of an older generation. And, we prayed. We prayed and we praised, and we prayed and we thanked God ahead of time for the miracle.

However, every month brought us disappointment. Mona's body wasn't responding to anything. Month after agonizing month came and went. An agonizingly slow year passed. It was a year of victories in many areas yet still we remained barren. Then, another year passed, even slower.

Our faith didn't waiver. Then, another few months passed, even slower. Incredibly, two years passed with my wife and I constantly praying to be able to conceive but us not to be able to do so. I refused to believe that God would not give us at least one child. So we kept praying and praising and believing.

Three years passed.

I was injecting my wife with needles filled with medicines designed to help grow follicles. We had tried just about everything we could. We were running out of options. But we kept on praising and praying and tithing and serving and singing and believing. I just knew God was setting all this up so that He could get the glory. I was cool with it, but I thought six months was sufficient and we would have given him all the glory even after three months, we were now going on three and a half years! Another month passed and yet another.

Four years passed. The doctors had already told us consider other options.

God opened the doors for her and I to travel to South Africa. The first time, I went alone. I met many wonderful people there. One such gentleman was Stephen Curle. A man

I had heard God used prophetically. I shared with him the situation Mona and I were in and he said, "If God ever opens the doors for me to meet her, I'd love to pray for her."

The following year, my wife was able to go to South Africa with me. True to his word, Mr. Stephen Curle and his prayer partner visited us at the hotel. The three of us began to pray for Mona, with Stephen laying hands on her head. Before we finished, she fell back, slain in the spirit. She was unresponsive for about half an hour. I prayed that God was on the move. That night, we made love.

When we went to our next scheduled doctors appointment, our doctor told us that a follicle – a single follicle – was starting to grow. He told us we had a limited window, three days, to try to get pregnant. So, we got busy on getting busy. The day I heard my beautiful wife was pregnant, I knew I was experiencing a Kairos Moment. It was a moment of answered prayers. Not only ours but also the many prayers many other people offered up on our behalf. I felt God validated our faithfulness. It was one of the best moments of my life.

Meeting Stephen Curle was a Kairos Relationship. Kairos Relationships are when God puts someone in your path for a season. Stephen and I didn't start a life-long, talk-once-a-week-on-the-phone type of relationship. I believe that God used him as the vessel to mark our lives, and not so much that he was meant to stay in our lives. Kairos Relationships can happen at any time. Those of us who seek to be in God's will are the ones God uses to mark others, sometimes as accountability partners and other times just for a season.

Now, I've heard it said that many men complain as much as the women when their women are pregnant. Sure, it's the woman's body that changes and with the weight gain, due to a new living creature being developed inside of them, their discomfort and pains illicit some complaint. By the way, complaints that they have every right to voice. But also, many men complain because their wives can no longer do for them what they used to before and… if I'm being honest, a lot of us men are big babies and when our wives can't do for us what we are used to, we cry like big babies too.

I however, couldn't complain. I was too grateful. My wife and I had struggled too long and too hard for me to complain. I took joy in telling her to sit back and relax as I rubbed her feet. I whistled while I cooked for her. I even sang when I would help with the laundry! We were pregnant! Life was great!

One day, while at my father's house, he observed Mona, who was starting to have a little difficulty breathing. He said to me. "Boy, you need to take your wife to the hospital. She's ready to go!"

At first I didn't think he could be right. The entire setting was far too calm. I was half-expecting a scene from a sitcom to materialize, sans the injected pre-recorded laughter. I expected for her to yell, "My water broke!" at the most inopportune time, quickly to be proceeded by pandemonium and chaos. Then I remembered that my father, Bishop Gideon Thompson, had 8 children of his own and had pastored for decades. I figured it was another good time to yield to his experience.

We got into the car, me in the driver's seat, my wife in the passenger's seat, and my mom in the back seat. As we were driving, with my wife practicing her newly acquired breathing technique, and with a little nervous excitement filling the vehicle, I drove over a bump. Shortly after, Mona said, "I think his head just popped out."

Okay. Let me pause here for a moment. To be driving through an ultra busy section of the crowded city of Boston (Hyde Park) and to hear your wife say, "I think his head just popped out," is one of the craziest and surreal moments I've ever experienced.

Then I saw something I had never seen before in the ultra-busy section of Hyde Park, three parking spots in a row were available, as if God wanted make sure I wouldn't miss them. I wasn't in the right mindset to appreciate God's perfect timing at the time, my son's head had just popped out!

After slamming on the brakes I hurried to the other side of the car. I had no idea what to do. Then, I remembered that my mother, a mother of 8 children of her own, was with us. I looked up to see if she would take over but she was nowhere in sight. I looked outside the car and saw her running up and down the street yelling, "My daughter is having a baby, someone help!"

This was a time when cell phones weren't very dependable and sure enough, my 9-1-1 call didn't get through. I was at a total loss. My wife was in the front seat of my car and the baby we had prayed for years for had just popped its head out way before we were ready for him. There were no nurses, no doctors, no epidurals, no heart monitors, no nothing. To top it off, the only person I thought capable of helping me was busy trying to flag down strangers for help!

Then, God showed up. It was as if, in an instant, He had downloaded into me exactly what to do. I calmly helped my wife put her seat back. As I began to help her with her pants, I felt the calming presence of the Holy Spirit and began speaking in tongues. I saw my son's head, it was purple and full of body fluids. A beautiful sight if I ever saw one. I held his head, instructed my wife to push and our baby boy started to enter into the world. By the time he was out, my mother was there, giving me a hand.

I took off my t-shirt and wrapped him up in it. My son, Matthew K Thompson Jr. lay on his mother's chest. The sounds of an ambulance grew louder until they parked right behind us. My mom turned out to be successful in getting someone to help! Mona was in a state of shock as the EMT's helped her on the gurney. My mother rode with them, hugging her newly born grandson with all her love. I drove behind the ambulance, not knowing how to name the feeling that had come over me. I could barely believe it, I was a father!

When we got there, the professionals took over. A nurse handed me the t-shirt I had used to wrap him with. I looked at it, focusing on the stains that proved my sons existence, the stains that proved God's faithfulness. When, suddenly, as if a mist had cleared, my eyes adjusted on the actual t-shirt itself. It was the t-shirt I had bought as a souvenir before leaving South Africa, where our pregnancy began due to a Kairos Moment.

## Winds of Change

There's a storm coming and I pray that this book, for you, becomes a spiritual Nor'easter. Those of us in New England know well what that is. Basically, it's a macro-scale cyclone. It thrives on converging air masses – the cold polar air mass over the cold ground and the warmer air over the

> **There's a storm coming**

water. The precipitation pattern is similar to that of other extra-tropical storms. Nor'easters are usually accompanied by very heavy rain or snow, and can cause severe coastal flooding, coastal erosion, hurricane-force winds, or blizzard conditions. It's almost like a perfect storm, containing with it attributes of many different storms.

I believe that in this season, God has decreed to induce a storm over your life that will challenge and shape you. I don't mean to say a storm as in a trial, per say. But a storm, a Nor'easter, if you will, designed to cover every area of your spiritual life. Causing within you severe coastal flooding (purging), coastal erosion (diminishing of yourself), hurricane force winds (knocking down the barriers that hinder your walk with Him), and blizzard conditions (a time to isolate yourself to focus on Him).

Jesus continued to say to Simon Bar-Jonah, who he had just named Peter – "And I will give you the keys of the kingdom of heaven, and whatever you bind on the earth will be bound in heaven, and whatever you loose on earth will be loosed in heaven."

Jesus gave us the keys, which implies that some things must be locked.

I pray that this book unlocks for you, not what you've been looking for, but that which God has ordained you to find.

*Dear reader, I have designed this book to be interactive, so that you can look back on what you have written in it and use it as a testimony to God's answer to your prayers. As you go through this book, there are a few sections designed for you to write in. I pray that you take advantage of these sections.*

What are the biggest or most memorable Kairos Moments you've experienced?

_____

_____

_____

_____

How have those moments shifted your life or impacted those around you?

_____

_____

_____

_____

## CHAPTER 2
# ATMOSPHERE

It's all around you. You can leave your house and it bids you
farewell, promising it'll be there when you get back, but at
the threshing floor, as soon as you get outside it greets you. You
can open the door to your car, think that you're now leaving it
outside but once you shut the door, it's there with you. You can
go to church. It's there. You can go to the store. You can go to
court. It's there. You can go to a sporting event, and it's there.

You can go to the ocean, dive 30ft down, and it's there.
You can zip yourself in a space suit, get on a space ship, and
leave the confines of this planet, and it's there. Not only is it in
the space ship, but it's also within your space suit! It's almost
always different, it takes on different 'personalities' if you will,
but it's there. Always.

Regardless of who you are, where you go, how much money
you make, how many times you pray, what nationality you are
– you are surrounded by atmosphere.

You need to understand this very important truth – most times, YOU decide the atmosphere around you. In your home, the place where most people spend the majority of their time, at work, with the people you choose to spend time with, in the place you congregate

> **YOU decide the atmosphere around you.**

with others to worship the name of the Lord – you have serious influence over the atmosphere you operate under.

Too many believers go through too many struggles and, unwittingly, many of their problems arise from the very atmosphere they create or choose to spend time under.

The teaching of 'Atmosphere' is multi-layered. There are many points I can make regarding this topic, however, the most important, by far, is to understand that God gave you the free will to create the atmosphere around you and your family.

## What creates an atmosphere?

What you do and say creates the atmosphere around you. Different rooms in your house exude different yearnings. For example, if you're in your garage, you might not be in the mood for snack or a drink, but if you go sit in your kitchen, you might find yourself biting into an apple or dunking a donut into a glass a of milk that you wouldn't have had, had you not switched rooms, switched atmospheres.

The real question you should ask yourself is, what sort of atmosphere are you building around you? I know for me and my house, who have decided to worship the Lord, the prevailing presence in my house is one of peace, communication, joy, and openness. The best way for Mona and I to create that type of atmosphere is by prioritizing prayer.

Let me preface what I'm about to say by first stating that prayer is powerful, regardless of where you do it. The act of speaking directly to God, whether you're driving, kneeling at the altar, or in your prayer closet at home, delivers miraculous outcomes. What I will say though, is this, to add a suitable place for prayer that enhances your time with God, makes your prayer time even more powerful. Many people put in their prayer time while driving. The problem with that is when you're driving and praying, you need to be cognizant of the road, pedestrians, and traffic. You're not focused on the God Almighty you are praying to. When you're kneeling at an altar, oftentimes there are other people there as well. If it's during an altar call there might be music and someone on a microphone.

Rooms have their own atmosphere, their own personalities, if you will. My kitchen has a prevailing atmosphere of food, community, laughter, creativity, and joy. My 'man-cave' has a prevailing atmosphere of competition, machismo, some good old fashion trash talking, light-heartedness, and, because I'm a Patriots fan, victory. My bedroom has a prevailing atmosphere of privacy, important marital conversations, security, and lovemaking.

When I pray in those rooms, obviously, it's not that God doesn't hear me, nor does it mean that I can't feel his presence – but due to the prevailing atmospheres associated with those rooms, it makes it a little harder for me to solely concentrate on His presence.

I believe that every believer should try to set up that one special place where you pray. The enemy has been quite successful at keeping people from recognizing the power of atmosphere, of creating a place were you can focus more intently on communicating with God. Think about the movie, War Room. Now, I'm not suggesting you use a closet, but if that's the only place in your home/apartment, by all means use the closet.

But I want to emphasize that God calls churches Houses of Prayer. God has spoken to me many times in my church. We hold, morning prayer there. When new pastors ask me for mentorship or guidance, I tell them to make sure that their church is a house of prayer. God has met me there.

> **God has met generations at Houses of Prayer around the world.**

God has met my father there. God has met my son there. God has met generations at Houses of Prayer around the world. I encourage you to take your petitions, your angst, your sufferings, your strife, your challenges, your hopes, your dreams, your plans, and bring them to a House of Prayer.

At Jubilee Church, as the senior pastor, I try to make sure that the only prevailing atmosphere is one where people hear from God. It's special to get a chance to speak to Him, but it's a life-changing Kairos Moment when He speaks to you or your situation.

## Blind Man in a Sports Car.

My father taught me long ago the importance of prayer. I grew up with him saying a story about a man in a lightning-quick sports car. His wife was about to give birth and he was on his way, going as fast as he could, to the hospital on top of a mountain. (Don't ask me why the hospital was on top of a mountain, I guess it's because it helps the analogy work better.) Anyway, the man is going up a winding two-lane road and he got behind a slow-moving 18-wheeler. Due to the constant turns, the man couldn't see too far ahead of him so he swerved a bit to his left, looking for a clear lane on the other side to pass the 18 wheeler. He quickly jerked his car back behind the 18-wheeler, barely missing another car going the other way. To his chagrin, traffic going the other way picked up. Every time he went to take a peak to see if he could pass the slow truck in front of him, he nearly crashed.

Overhead was a man in a helicopter. He could tell that the man couldn't see far enough in front of him to make the pass. He wished he could communicate with the man in the sports car, to tell him that he could see everything clearly, that he could see what the driver of the car couldn't. If he could only communicate with him, he would tell him when the coast was clear, when to 'punch it' and pass the 18-wheeler.

And in a way, that's how God must feel with us. He sees us trying to make moves, or scared to make a move, and he'd love to communicate with us, to tell us – "I see everything, I'm the Alpha and Omega. If you would just communicate

**I see everything, I'm the Alpha and Omega.**

with me and trust me, I can direct your path to the place you need to be." However, like the man in the sports car, we remain isolated and thus, miss out on many birthings.

## The Influence of Atmospheres

I went to a Patriots game with my son a little while back. Not just any game, a playoff game against the rival Steelers. I didn't wear my Pastor shoes, I didn't have my Pastor Bible, and I didn't bring my armor bearer. I was there, as a fan, a man and his son, prepared to root for the home team. We were decked out in Patriots gear and blended right in.

The game was very competitive. Everyone in the stadium was charged up. On my way back from the concession stand, the guy that stood up to let me in our row put an arm out, halting my progress.

"Listen guy," he said, the odor from him told me that he had ordered from a different concession stand than me. "Can you believe we have a Steelers fan in our row?"

The way he said it was as if it was an affront to him, and it should have been to me. Without realizing it, I answered. "No way! In OUR row?"

"I, for one, aint gonna stand for it." Then he leaned in, "By the end of this game, I'm gonna take him out. Can I count on you?"

I looked at him, me, Pastor Matthew K Thompson, and yelled out, "Ya, let's take him out!"

As I made my way to my seat, I scanned the row for the traitorous person who dared defy Patriot Nation by wearing another team's Jersey. By the time I sat down, I was shocked and appalled. *Wait. What... What just happened? What did I just agree to?"*

The game finished with the Steeler fan sore from losing but still alive. I think the guy who ordered the hit had visited that one concession stand a few more times and forgot about it. But what stood out to me, as I reflected back on that day was how powerful the atmosphere around us can be. I made a declaration, *"Let's take him out!"* I never thought I would ever utter. The atmosphere had gotten the better of me.

In middle school (Jr. High School) and High School, atmospheres are sometimes created when two kids argue and then suddenly they're surrounded by a group of people yelling, "Fight! Fight! Fight!"

In churches all across the country and in many parts of the world, atmospheres are created when the assembled saints lift their voices in song, in one accord, to praise the lord. The atmosphere allows us the freedom to raise our hands and shout praises to God, a freedom we don't experience at our secular jobs. Atmospheres are vital spiritual weapons and if you could learn to harness the power of the right atmosphere, God can do greater things in you and through you.

## The Problem with Free

As I work on this book, I do so with a burden to convince you on how powerful connecting with God is. Prayer needs to be a priority in your life if you want to have victory over your flesh and over the principalities that govern this fallen world. By establishing the right atmosphere, God can communicate with you better. He can tell you to slow down, to speed up, to turn right, to pull over and get some sleep, and when to pull over and pick up a passenger.

I don't believe that many Christians value the ability to speak with God as much as they should. Seriously, the fact that He gave us prayer is beyond amazing. But, since, for us, it doesn't come with a price, many of us don't realize its value. We'll do almost anything instead of praying. We'll jog, we'll binge-watch on Netflix, we'll get on social media, we'll shoot hoops, we'll golf, we'll shop, we'll read; we'll do just about anything instead of spend time in prayer. Now, some of you might think that I'm being a little facetious here, like I'm making another analogy.

I'm not. I'm dead serious.

How many times have you turned on the television this week in comparison to the times you've knelt down before the Lord in prayer? How many hours have you spent on social media sites in comparison to prayer? How much time did you spend at the gym, stores, or playing free games on your phone in comparison to praying? Your actions are the manifestations of your priority list.

> **Your actions are the manifestations of your priority list.**

Jesus, the Christ, paid a hefty price to give us instant access to God, the Father. Oh, if God's people all across this country would understand what a gift prayer is. And how humbling it is to have it.

I have had the privilege of meeting some great men and women of God. I've been in the company of spiritual leaders known far and wide. Whenever I'm in their presence, in the presence of people with years of wisdom and divine revelation, I don't talk nearly as much. I don't even waste my breath. I already know what I know. I want to know what they know!

For a period of time I felt in awe of these people, if I'm being honest, I still do. To have their sole attention and speak to me and pour into me was an honor I felt I didn't deserve. One day, I felt God ask me, "When was the last time you respected me like you do them?"

Here I am, with the ability to communicate with God in prayer, and I'm getting giddy about speaking with His servants. (No disrespect intended to the mighty men of God I still admire).

Now, if any of these men wanted to come to my house for dinner, I'd make sure the entire house was clean, top to bottom, I'd make sure the menu was top-notch, in short, I would go out of my way to create an atmosphere that would make them comfortable. But I hadn't necessarily gone out of my way to do the same for God. Ouch! God let me understand that I needed to create an atmosphere where He can manifest His presence from inside my home.

When was the last time the president or former president of the United States said he wanted to come to your home? I have great news for you. Someone much grander is seeking an audience with you. Create a place, a special place, where the presence of the All Mighty God, the King of Kings, the Lord of Lords, the Great I Am, the Alpha, the Omega, the Creator of all; a place where Jehovah Himself can enter into true dialogue with you.

## Simple Prayer

It starts with prayer. Simple prayer.

Naturally, I joke when I say 'simple prayer.' Prayer is anything but simple. I don't know anything about 'Simple Prayer.'

**Prayer is anything but simple.**

I know about Dynamic, Heart Changing Prayer.
I know about Generational-Curse Breaking prayer.
I've been witness to Miraculous Healing Prayer.

I've seen Addiction-Ending Prayer.

I have partaken in I-Don't-See-A-Way-Out-But-He-Made-a-Way-Out Prayer.

God is calling you into a deeper relationship with Him. I pray that you receive this in your spirit. There's a higher dimension of authority you are meant to walk in. You don't have to hear about Him. You don't have to look up YouTube videos of Him. You don't have to wait for a time to catch Him on TV. All you have to do is prioritize prayer time with Him.

Jesus said, "When you pray..." If you're still on *if* and not on *when,* you have a lot of spiritual growing to do.

The disciples asked him, "Teach us to pray." See, they had seen God do all sorts of miracles through Jesus. But they also saw him get up early and often to pray. They knew the secret was prayer but they didn't know how to do it. Child of God, I can't make this clear enough – the road to victory is paved with prayer.

Exercise the authority you have in your home and establish a place where you pray to Him. Remove all distractions when you pray. Create an atmosphere of freedom and peace through the power of prayer. Pray with faith. Pray with valor. Pray with your heart. Pray with your soul. Pray with tears. Pray with a feeling of expectation. Pray with gladness. Pray with boldness. Validate what you say you believe in and pray.

When the prevailing atmosphere in your home is prayer... all will be a witness to what God can do through you.

How can you create a more Godly Atmosphere in your home?

_____

_____

_____

_____

Where will you establish a place of prayer in your home?

_____

_____

When is the next time you will dedicate prayer time at your church?

_____

_____

## CHAPTER 3
# THE POWER OF WHY

Many times, for things of importance, or rather, for there to be consistency in a new action, such as changing ones diet or learning a new skillset, the *why* of it needs to be uniquely important for the individual. If someone starts a diet because they saw themselves in a mirror and realized they didn't like what they saw, the odds are against them in them getting to their goal weight or size. If there is one reason why people don't lose weight its because their reason(s) for doing so are not stronger than the temptation they face from foods they swore they wouldn't eat.

Most people that struggle losing weight blame it on the diet and, switch diets. "That diet didn't work for me." Yet, they rarely have success, regardless of what diet they choose. The problem isn't the diet they subscribe to, the problem lies in their reasons to lose the weight. The problem isn't that the class is too difficult, it's that their reasons for passing the class aren't strong enough for them to pay attention and do the homework. The problem isn't that starting a business is too difficult, it's that their reasons for working for themselves doesn't motivate them enough to risk them not having the steady paycheck they're used to. The problem isn't that playing the piano is too difficult, it's that their reason for being a musician isn't strong enough for them to spend hours practicing.

The diet industry is a multi-billion dollar industry because people lack willpower. People fail over and over again, which means the industry gets repeat clients. Willpower is fueled by a person's reason to do something; on their, *why*.

Imagine this:

- If your doctor told you that if you don't lose at least twenty pounds in the next 4 months, due to the diabetes you have because of your poor eating choices, you're going to lose your toes...
- If your parents told you that if you got straight-A's they would buy you a brand new car for your senior year of high school...
- If you knew that in two years you would make twice as much money as a business owner than an employee...
- If you knew that your favorite singer wanted to hire you to be his/her piano player...

You would be more likely to push through those moments that typically derail you. Your *why* would be important enough to force you to accept a new normal, a new routine, a new eating plan, or new study habits.

That is the power of why. Humans need it. Ever since Adam and Eve bit into the fruit of knowledge, we as a species have been driven by our *whys*. If we don't know why to do something, we won't do it.

> **If we don't know why to do something, we won't do it.**

The strength and authenticity of our *why* determines if we decide to do something or not.

In chapter 2, I spoke about prayer not being high enough on people's priority lists. I hope it got you thinking about how you spend your time; hour after hour, day after day. If you know you need to spend more time in prayer I hope it convicted you. Many of us have been there, thinking that we need to pray more. Just like many have thought they need to lose weight.

Can it be that God's chosen people, His bride, His church, doesn't have a powerful enough *why to pray* and that's why some of His children pray once a week or once a month? Maybe it's because you pray weekly or monthly that you find yourself struggling against the same demons and challenges you've been fighting with for 20 years? Don't you want to be free?

My goal is to inspire you to pray more, to help you find your reason for prayer.

## Real Prayer Warriors

Like Paul and Silas, when they were imprisoned, many of us were or are in bondage. At around midnight, a time where bad things tend to happen, they started singing and praying. When I read their story, at first it didn't make sense to me. Who gets happy from losing their freedom?

As my knowledge in God grew, I understood that they didn't sing because they were happy they were in jail, they sang because they were happy to know God. They didn't allow their current circumstance to impede them from feeling the love of God. It didn't matter where they were, they were going to sing. They had joy in the Lord. They were profoundly in love with His presence.

It sort of reminds me of the way young lovers feel for each other. Back in the day, before cell phones, they would be trapped sitting on the kitchen table, or wherever the phone was stuck to the wall, and just love talking to the other person. It made no difference if the kitchen chair was made of wood and devoid of any cushion, they would sit there for hours, basking in the attention of the other person. When the time came for them to hang up, they would politely and respectfully argue for the other person to get off the phone first.

"Ok, hang up now. I love you."

"No, you hang up."

"I can't. You do it."

Neither wanted to hang up because they did not want to be the reason why the conversation stopped. Such, was their love, some call it Puppy Love.

I remember when Mona and I were dating, I would be sitting there, in bliss, talking softly into the phone, trying to be cool. I didn't realize it at the time but I was trying to create an atmosphere, through the phone lines of trust, intimacy, longing, and desire – and people would come into the room talking to me all loud, totally destroying the mood. I would put my hand over the phone and yell at them in my loudest whisper, "Leave me alone. I'm on the phone!"

I wanted her to have my undivided attention. I couldn't get enough of her. I needed to know more of her, as much as I could.

If we could all be so focused on God, like Paul and Silas were. They weren't just in prison, they weren't just in a cell, they were chained up in a cell. That's like prison squared (multiplied by 2). Not only could they not leave, but if they got an itch on their back, they couldn't scratch it. Anybody else would be feeling sorry for him or herself. *I can't believe I'm here. I don't deserve to be here. This is so unfair.*

What impresses me most about them singing is that shortly before being imprisoned, the bible says a multitude rose up against them. (Oh I can go on and on about people's need to be popular but I'll just move on) Then the magistrate commanded the people to beat them. Acts 16, verse 23 - In the King James Version, "And when they had laid many stripes upon them, they cast them into prison." Translation for, Laid Many Stripes Upon Them = they beat them to a pulp, gave them an old-fashioned whoopin', beat the living daylights out of them.

Yet, there they sat, bloodied and beaten but glad to serve the King of Kings. I would think that if someone asked Paul how he was doing he might've answered, "I'm blessed and highly favored." You see, they didn't judge their relationship with God based on their current situation. They had a

**They didn't judge their relationship with God based on their current situation.**

personal encounter with God and were so much in love with Him that nothing could keep them from praising Him.

Suddenly, there was a great earthquake so strong it shook the very foundations of the prison. And immediately all the doors were opened and everyone's shackles were loosed.

## Find your, *Why*

If you need a reason to pray, if you need a *why,* look at what God did there. He shook the very foundations of the place that imprisoned them. Not only did the shackles fall off of them, but also off everyone who heard them praying and singing!

Prayer is the main ingredient to victorious living. Paul and Silas were in need of a supernatural occurrence and God showed up in a mighty way.

I want to challenge you to get your prayer life going. Activate the supernatural power of God to move on your behalf. It works. As a believer first and then a Pastor, I've heard testimony after testimony of God shaking foundations and loosening shackles. If you travel to spirit-filled churches all over the world, you would hear testimonies of answered prayers.

God can't answer your prayer if you don't offer it up. Many people's problem is not the unanswered prayer, it's the unoffered prayer. If you have a child that doesn't serve the Lord, get a prayer life. If

> **Many people's problem is not the unanswered prayer, it's the unoffered prayer.**

you don't know what to do professionally, get a prayer life. If your marriage is in trouble, get a prayer life. If you're sick, get a prayer life. If you love your job, get a prayer life. If your marriage is going great, get a prayer life. Not only will God loosen some shackles on your life, more importantly, your prayers loosen the shackles on God to work on your behalf.

In order for you to fulfill the destiny God has for you here on earth, whether it's in a church, in ministry, in your family, in your community or in your profession, get a prayer life! For whatever is important to you, pray. And then pray and then pray some more.

## Just Do It

Now let's talk about the how.

When you are a new believer, in my opinion, how you pray doesn't matter that much. We talk how we talk. Getting saved doesn't come with a perfect vocabulary and King James-style language. However, based on the characteristics of God, particularly in the Old Testament, there is a level of reverence that God appreciates. While I don't think you need to pray with words like "thou" and "art" and "whom," I also believe that when seeking an audience the all mighty God, that you don't talk to him exactly like you do everyone else.

I think the creator of heaven and earth should be spoken to differently than how you speak to your "homie." It's not the language that's wrong with certain types of prayer, we speak how we speak, it's the lack of respect and humility, the absence of praise and adoration that God delights in.

But I would imagine that, however you speak to Him in prayer, it gives Him extreme pleasure. As you grow in your Christian walk, the right words will come.

Jesus taught us how to pray. The problem is, too many people pray it but don't understand the *why* behind it. Turn the page and let's take a close look at the Lord's Prayer.

# CHAPTER 4
# THE LORD'S PRAYER

Our father, who art in heaven, hallowed
be thy name.
Thy Kingdom come, thy will be done.
On earth, as it is in Heaven.
Give us this day our daily bread.
And forgive us our debts, as we forgive
our debtors.
And lead us not into temptation, but deliver us
from evil.
For yours is the kingdom, and the power, and
the glory, for ever. Amen.

In Matthew 6: 9-13, we see Jesus teaching his disciples (and
the billions of his followers throughout history) how to
pray. I've prayed it. My wife has prayed it. My dad has prayed
it. Billions of people, maybe including you, have prayed it.
Some people have prayed it so often, it has stopped serving as

a prayer and has instead become a ritual. Something you say from memory, not with heart, soul, pleading, gratitude, passion, or desire. People have been playing a spiritual "Simon Says" game with the Lord's prayer, thus dare I say, to many, it has lost its potency.

The good news is, I don't think it was Jesus' intent for us to learn to recite "his prayer" ritualistically. But I do think it's incredibly powerful. I have found that it contains a spiritual formula that allows us to touch the very heart of God. The formula is hidden in its simplicity.

## The Formula

I believe that the all-knowing God has revealed insight of this prayer to many people and in different forms. I'll tell you what He has revealed to me in praying, The Lord's Prayer.

## Our Father, who art in heaven.

We start the prayer by honoring him, calling him, Father. A father is the primary leader of a family and protector of his children. It's the father's surname that attaches itself to the son or daughter. The bible teaches that the father is the head of the house. So when we start the prayer by calling him father, we let Him know that we know our roles.

We also let him know that we know that He is above us, in heaven. By referencing heaven; a place with streets of gold, a place where the angels sing praises to him, a place of peace, joy, and abundant love... we acknowledge its existence. It demonstrates our faith and belief in His word.

## Hallowed be thy name

The word, *hallow,* means, honor as holy, greatly revered or respected. So we say, "Lord, I respect you. I revere your very name. Your name implies greatness, awesomeness, and holiness." He likes that. If you don't believe me, you haven't read your bible enough. Our God loves to be praised. He inhabits within the praises of His children.

In essence, when I start to pray, I start by praising more than praying. The word prayer has a connotation of requesting or asking. When I start communicating with God, I don't get into ask-mode first, I get into praise-mode.

**I start by praising more than praying.**

I tell Him that I know how amazing He is and I'm humbled that I get a chance to speak with Him. I talk to him out of reverence and respect. I don't tell someone, "You're an amazing singer" if they're just average. I won't tell my son, "You played a great basketball game." if he went 1-for-12 with three turnovers and fouled out. My compliments come from a place of truth. When I pray, I open up the compliment treasure chest and heap praise upon praise to the God that saved a wretched sinner like me.

I love it. I love to praise Him. He is worthy, He has been worthy since the beginning of time, and He will continue to be worthy of being praised. Regardless of what happens to me, He will be worthy of being praised. If I lose everything but have my Father's love, He's worthy to be praised. So, again, when I start to pray I don't pray, I worship his name.

## Thy Kingdom come. They will be done.

Matthew 6: 33 "But seek first his kingdom and his righteousness, and all these things will be given to you as well."

I tell God that I long to do His will for His kingdom. That I'm concerned about what He's concerned about. There's a song we sing in our church, part of the lyrics go, "Open the eyes of my heart Lord, so I can see you." It's a wonderful song of worship. When I pray, I take it a step further. I pray that God opens the eyes of my heart so I can see like He sees.

I ask the Lord to use me for His kingdom, His glory. I put myself at His disposal. To use me to help shift the atmospheres I encounter. To put me in play, to trust me enough to put me into the game, that His will is my will, that I want whatever He wants. I want to be a representation of Him on earth so I ask Him to allow that to happen.

## On earth, as it is in Heaven

I'll admit, it took a while for His discernment to penetrate into my carnal mind on this part. The cynic in me, the inquisitive part of me that sometimes doesn't allow me to take many things at face value, had a hard time believing how it could be possible that Heaven invades the earth.

The people of earth have made it so divisive, controversial, and dangerous. Heaven is a place with no poverty, no prejudice, no pain, and no violence… I couldn't fathom why Jesus would teach us to pray, "On earth as it is in Heaven" when they are total opposites.

But that's where faith comes in. It's during that part of the prayer that I recall when Jesus asked his disciples, "Who do men say I am?" and Peter answered that he is the son of the living God. Then the Lord revealed to Peter that on him, he would be the rock he would build the foundation for the message of salvation for all of humanity and that the gates of hell would not prevail against it. And I pray for God to bestow upon me divine revelation to things I can't see, to things I can't comprehend, to things that are too intricate or complex for my human, finite mind to fathom.

I once spoke to a friend and told him I was praying for him. What he said shocked me.

"Save your breath."

"Why would you say that?" I asked.

"I'm not going to heaven. I'm going to hell." He meant it. "In fact, I'm living in hell right now. I'm sick, my body is breaking down from the inside. My relationship with every one of my children is shattered; they don't want anything to do with me. I'm going through hell right now."

God revealed to me that if that man could experience hell on earth, it's possible for people to experience heaven on earth. Heaven on earth for me is to know that my wife loves the Lord and that my children are saved. There was a period of time in my life when I wondered if my daughter would ever come to know God in a real way. She went through hell... but that's just it. She went through it, she didn't stay stuck in it. A day of salvation came to her life that marked her and shifted her destiny.

To know that for me and my house, and the people really important to me, who I love like family, that we all serve the Lord, is like heaven on earth. When I greet the members and visitors that attend our services, and I see their smiles and can feel their warmth, that's heaven on earth to me. When I hear that a prayer request has been answered, that's heaven on earth for me.

Having that peace that defies logic, or as the Bible puts it, surpasses all understanding, is heaven on earth. When you should be worried about the report from your doctor, but instead you're singing a hymn as you put your Sunday shoes on to go to church, when you should be worried about getting the loan but instead you're out shopping for where your office is going to be, when your enemies rise up against you and your haters come out of the woodwork and you've lost your job and you don't know how you're going to pay your rent and your last good friend turned her back on you and you only have half a loaf of bread and a jar of peanut butter in your cupboard – BUT YOU STAND TALL AND RAISE YOUR HANDS AND GIVE THANKS TO GOD FOR ALL HE'S GIVEN YOU – that's experiencing heaven on earth when anyone else would experience hell.

It's when in the bad times you don't yell and don't cry, but instead you say to the principalities of this world, "Yea, though I walk through the valley of the shadow of death, I will fear no evil, I know my redeemer lives. I know God is with me. He has prepared a table before me in the presence of my enemies, and just like He said to Joshua, they won't be able to stand against me. He has anointed me in oil and covered me with the blood of Christ Jesus. Surely goodness and mercy shall

**I know my redeemer lives.**

follow me and come hell or high water, I will remain a servant of the one true God and dwell in the house of the Lord forever." That's living heaven on earth.

I believe it's a part of our responsibility as believers to pray for an Open Heaven. For the floodgates of blessings to pour down, for forgiveness to defeat stubbornness, and for God's glory to reveal itself far and wide. At Jubilee Church we each have a card with five names on it. We are all praying for those five people whose names appear on each card. We pray and proclaim they get to know Jesus the savior and God the father. So that they too can experience heaven on earth.

## Give us this day our daily bread

At one point of Jesus' life on earth, he found himself in a huge battle. The father of lies and deception was tempting him. His body was weak but his spirit was strong. Satan appealed to his flesh, to his need to survive, "If you're the Son of God, turn these stones into bread. I know you're starving. You haven't eaten in 40 days. You're not a commoner. You fasted your 40 days. You're hungry, why should you wait another second to eat?"

Jesus blasted him with scripture. "Man shall not live by bread alone but by every word that proceeded out of the mouth of God."

In other words, he told the devil, "You misunderstand me Satan. You just don't get it. You never did get it. You misunderstand creation. It's not bread that my decaying body needs, it's to be in the presence of God. It's to hear His words."

I don't know about you but I don't take days off without eating. In the same way, I don't take a day off without digesting God's word. I have daily needs, I face daily battles, and I need a daily dosage of that good stuff that only God can give me. I ask God to help me in specific areas. I mention to Him my worries and doubts, and ask that He be the one involved in my future plans.

I then pray for the people on my prayer list. Our daily bread doesn't have to be solely on our wants and needs. I start with my family. On Mondays, Wednesdays, and Friday's I pray for my family. I start with my wife, Mona, and I get to my children, grandchildren, and parents. That usually takes more than just Monday. But during the week I move on to my siblings and their immediate families.

On Tuesdays and Thursdays I pray for people outside of my family. Members of my church, people in leadership, people I've come across that God puts in my heart on certain occasions, and the people I know who are lost. I pray by name and by need. I stand in the gap for those that need it. In faith I proclaim the promises of Jesus over their lives. Praying for others typically takes up the longest portion of my prayer time.

## Forgive us our debt, as we forgive our debtors

I thank Him, thank Him, and thank Him for saving me. Sometimes, this can go on for quite a while. Then I pray to be able to live with a forgiving heart. I pray that He wash me, cleanse me, and restore me. I want to be able to walk in fellowship and unity. I cry out for Him to give me the power to love my neighbor as myself. Trust me, it's a powerful thing to be able to forgive and I want to wield it.

The power to forgive brings about the ability to live in freedom. It allows me to be excited and expectant about my future instead of defeated by my past.

## Lead us not into temptation but deliver us from evil.

If you're a parent with younger children, I share your struggle. This younger generation is growing up in a world far more distracting than ours. Sin is easier and more convenient than ever before. Evil lurks in apps, games, social statuses, online, in person, at school, at the park, and even at church. Temptation is all around us like never before in history. In our phones we carry around the ability to view pornography, to join cheating dating sites, to gamble, and to access people from all over the world.

> **Evil lurks in apps, games, social statuses, online, in person, at school, at the park, and even at church.**

I pray vehemently for God to protect my children from the lure of addictions. I pray He strengthen them and whenever they find themselves weak, that He deliver them. I call upon 1st Corinthians 10 verse 13 that states that God will always allow a way of escape from temptation. I pray that my children seek the way out, find it, and use it.

However, I don't just pray for things we struggle against, I pray for the types of doors that will present themselves, that we have the correct discernment to see which ones to walk through and which ones to close. That we understand the difference as a church between the ministries we are called to act on and the ministries we are good at. I pray for the colleges and universities that will accept my son, I pray that he choose the one God would have him attend.

## For yours is the Kingdom, and the power, and the glory for ever and ever. Amen.

I start praying by praising God and I finish by praising God. In my heart, I'm letting Him know that these are my requests and I hope He finds it in His will to answer them the way I would want them answered. But by ending up praising Him, I tell the King of Kings, regardless of how He elects to answer my requests, He is still my God and I will still serve Him. He is still just and He is still worthy of my praise. He is the epitome of victory and glory and at the end of the day, I'm just happy to be called, son.

### Let Him Talk

I felt the Lord tell me once, "When are you going to give me the chance to speak?" So now, before I'm done, sometimes I'll put on some worship music and meditate on His word. I have done all I could to make His presence prevalent in my home. I have designated a place for prayer where I'm free from distractions so that my mind can get as clear as I can make it so that my soul can better communicate with God. I ask that He direct my thoughts and ask that He reveal to me what His desire is from and for me.

For the most part, that's how I pray. If you were keeping score, I'll make it easy for you. In a nutshell, this is how I interpret the Lord's Prayer:

- Start by praising him
- Ask Him to use you for His will
- Get in a spirit of expectancy, for miracles
- Pray for specific needs
- Pray for your family
- Pray for those closest to you and those on your prayer list
- Pray for those you know are lost
- Thank Him for forgiving you
- Pray for a forgiving heart and mindset
- Pray protection over your family
- Pray that He open and close the doors ahead of you
- End by praising Him
- Then meditate, and allow Him to speak to you.

I'm not saying that this is the only way to pray but I will say that this is typically how I pray. I can tell you it has worked for me. I am humbled to say I have witnessed God move mountains on my behalf. The power of praise and prayer, like when Paul and Silas did when they were in prison, really shifts an atmosphere.

It is my belief that God will reveal to some who read this chapter, on what they need to pray about and specific people they need to stand in the gap and pray for. For that reason, please utilize this section for notes. If God has put someone in your heart or mind right now, write his or her name down in this section. If He put a need or cause in your heart, write it down here as well. Then pray over it. Offer up praise and prayer to God right now. Dare to move His heart and watch Him respond.

I believe that, as you read this chapter or as you read this right now, God has put someone or some situation in your heart. I believe God wants you to pray on whatever or whoever it is. Write the name of the person or the situation here on the notes section. Then write a prayer to God. Then read it out loud with faith that He hears you.

Name of person or situation: _____

Name of person or situation: _____

Name of person or situation: _____

Your Prayer:

_____

_____

_____

_____

_____

_____

Date: _____

Unfortunately, I don't think that everyone will fill out this section. Before you move on, I encourage you to trust that God has a plan with you through this book. Fill this section out. I believe it will serve as proof to a testimony you will share in the future.

## CHAPTER 5

# THE GOOD FATHER

## Names of God

There are many names for God. Truth be told, he's a God of many names. El-Shaddai, Yahweh, The Great I Am, Elohim, Jehovah, Jehova Jire, Jehovah Nissi, Jehova Shaalom, Jehovah Rapha, Jehovah, Shammah, Jehova Sabaoth, Adonai, King of Kings, Lord of Lords, Lord of Hosts, Ancient of Days, Alpha and Omega, and potentially many others. One of the ones he's most referred to is, Father. Or, to be more biblically correct, Abba Father, which means Most High Father. And when you pray, he'll answer to any of these names because all of them are Him and He is all of them. He is, after all, the Most High God.

However, when it comes to God being referred to as father, it puts a different connotation to our relationship with him. All of the other names we have for Him are grandiose, as if He is way out of our league. And He is. The creator is much more evolved than the creation. But when we reference him as *Father,* it almost has a way of humanizing Him.

When I hear the word, father, I don't immediately think of the Lord of Hosts, I think of Bishop Gideon Thompson. I don't actually go around calling him Bishop Gideon Thompson, most times I just call him dad. And when I pray to my father in heaven, I think of the Supreme Being I live to serve. *Our father, who art in heaven, hallowed be thy name...*

But, as a Pastor, I've noticed that not everyone can differentiate between the father in heaven and their father on earth. People's perspectives of what a father means, based on how their father by blood has been to them, actually hinders their ability to see God for who He truly is, or better put, to see God as Abba Father.

There's a dilemma of fatherlessness in many communities across the globe. Many people's ideas of fathers are tied to feelings of abandonment and rejection. Too many men have created children and have cowardly left them to be raised by their mother's, who at times, bring in other males to be their "father figures." Conversely, too many children see their mothers also as fathers, so their views on fatherhood is skewed because they are shown how to be a father from a females perspective of a male instead of a being shown how to be a father from an actual male.

Abandonment doesn't always necessarily means that the father has run off. It can also mean that the father is out working too often and when he does come home he doesn't have the energy or the desire to spend the amount of time with a child that the child craves. So, for this and other reasons, when many people think of the term father, a negative construct permeates their senses.

Thank God for mothers. We had a father who was constantly on the road, using his gifts to provide for the family. My mother, a true woman of prayer and faith, held our family together. She made sure to make sure we ate, bathed, rested, and got along. My father rarely gave me what I wanted, not because he didn't want to, but because he either didn't know what I wanted or we didn't have the means of getting me what I wanted. We didn't grow up dirt poor but we were far from rich. And although my dad would rarely give me what I wanted, he always gave me what I needed.

As I got older, I relied less on him. He had so many mouths to feed and as an elder sibling, I tried to take care of myself as soon as I could. At around that time I started to make a shift from my reliance on my dad to a reliance on my heavenly father. You could say that my younger siblings; April, Joel, Michael, and Debbie had a different father than I did. Of course, it was the same great man but his ministry was better established so he was home much more often. They grew up in ministry and in a household that was financially better equipped.

When Debbie came of age to go to college, she chose Berklee College of Music. Due to my dad's sowing, planning, and hard work she didn't have to think to herself, *how will I be able to afford college?* It was quite different for me when, years before, I contemplated college. I was fortunate enough to apply and receive the Project Reach Scholarship and also got a partial basketball scholarship to play at Morehouse College. Even though my dad has always been there for me and has bestowed blessings upon me and has been my biggest cheerleader, there was only so much he, or any human father could do.

## Father God

I'd like to sit with you here a moment to share with you more of who God, The Father, really is.

The first thing we need to know is that God is not bound by space and time. Nor is He bound by gravity. He is not influenced by the weather or popular opinion. He doesn't succumb to illnesses or accidents. And He certainly is not governed by human laws. God is also not bound by earthly family hierarchies.

When a man has a son or daughter, he becomes a father. When that son has a child, he then becomes a father and his father becomes a grandfather. When the grandson has a son, the original father becomes a great grandfather and his son becomes a grandfather.

In our family makeups, we hold many titles. Males are son. We are Father. We become grandfather. And if we're lucky, we become great grandfather. We are also brother, cousin, second cousin, and many people's favorite – we are uncle. Each of those titles brings with it different roles. You don't act like a son to your son, you act like a father. You don't act like a grandfather to your brother, you act like a brother. So our family hierarchy oftentimes dictates the roles we play in them. (Naturally, women have their titles as well but for the point I want to make here, I'm going to keep it male-centric.)

It's interesting to note that, in this day and age when we can – to copy the popular Burger King slogan – *have it our way*, we have very little say in the family titles we are given. We have no say in being a brother, uncle, or cousin. It's out of our control. Yet, in a harmonious family, the circumstances that are out of our control dictate to us how we function within our immediate and extended family.

But none of those rules apply to God the father being that He is not a man nor a son of man. God is not subjected to family roles. He is not governed by marriages or lineages. God has never been son. God has never been cousin. God has never been uncle. And God has never been grandfather.

When someone starts playing an instrument or a sport, they're usually not good at it on the onset. After a while, if they don't improve fast enough for their liking, they might put down the guitar and try the piano, or they might put down the basketball and start throwing a football. But the people that get really good, I mean world-class good, are people that stick to their instrument or sport and practice it over and over and over again. At one point in time they can be the best in the world, but because we succumb to time, there's a point when they can't get any better and they start regressing.

No matter how good they get, there comes a point in time when they can't get any better. Age becomes a factor and the fingers don't move as fast and the legs don't run as fast. It's usually at around that time that their mental IQ's relating to their sport or instrument advances beyond what their physical bodies are capable of doing.

Time does not affect God.

God doesn't regress at being a father. He's been father since before time began. Jesus has been son since time began. God has been father to his creation since he created it. He's been father to billions and billions. I dare say that God has gotten really good at being a father. The thing about God is, unlike us when our bodies get weary and we can't get

> **God has gotten really good at being a father.**

any better, God remains all-knowing and all-powerful. No disrespect to any great father's out there but, frankly, we can never measure up to the fatherhood styling's of the Great I Am.

I'd like for you to truly understand why He is called the Most High Father so allow me to drive the point home. Just as a human can become an expert at something, with 20, 30, or 50 years of experience, imagine how amazingly incredible an omnipotent being can be when he has done something for centuries!

It is to that father that I pray to. It is of that father I preach about. It is that father that I want to emulate. It is that father that I long to spend time with. It is that father that I hope you come to know in a real way.

To any of you who do not have a stellar recollection of your father, or who never knew your father, or who have a legitimate gripe against your father, I want to free you of comparing that father to our heavenly one. The earth is the Lord's and everything in it and He will bless you according to His will and riches in glory.

## Play Date

Being a father is a hugely important role. The only role as important to a child is being a mother. No other title can compare to those. In our house, we take those roles seriously. We're the type of parents that accompany our children on "play dates."

Years ago, my son's friend invited him over to his house to hang out. (I doubt they called it a play date!) Mona and I played Rocks, Papers, Scissors and I lost so I accompanied Matty to his friend's house. When we arrived, the boy's father opened the door and greeted us warmly. After Matty said hello and ran in, the man assured me that Matty would be taken care of and well fed and politely went to shut the door. I stuck my foot in the doorway and politely informed him that while Matty was there, his dad would be there also. I didn't know the atmosphere of the house. I didn't know what they believed. I didn't know the type of language they spoke behind closed doors. So I had to be present to protect my son from a potentially harmful atmosphere.

Being that I always have work to do, as every other Pastor I know, I told the man that he didn't have to entertain to me,

"If you could just give me a place where I can sit and plug in my laptop, I'll be fine."

I remember the room he put me in vividly because in front of the back wall was a large fish tank filled with water but devoid of any fish. Apparently the filter was broken and asking for help because every 45 seconds it blared out a little high-pitched beep. As time dragged on, that cute little beep became an incredibly annoying noise. When the beep wasn't going off, the man, in the next room, was typing something and every time he hit the return key I could hear a click. The beep and click wouldn't have been so bad if it were in synch like a beat but the timing of the two were grossly disjointed. Also, and I assure you I'm not making this up, the man was probably hard of hearing because his television was very loud. To make matters worse, they were cat people and their two cats thought I was the most interesting thing in the world because one kept staring at me and the other kept coming up to me. It even dared to jump on my lap! Probably not a big deal for some but I'm a dog guy so I wasn't thrilled to be the center of all that feline attention.

So there I was, trying to concentrate on my work but I had an incessant beeping going on, a clicking going on at random intervals, a television blaring, a cat staring at me without blinking and another cat jumping all over me when I vaguely heard a voice cry out, "Daddy!"

I jumped up, scaring the daylights out of both cats, and ran to where my son was. I nearly kicked the door down not knowing what to expect. But my son was there playing with his friend. He only had one care in the world.

"Dad, I'm hungry." He said, barely looking up at me.

On the way home, I let myself feel good for parenting my son's play date. (I'll admit, I also felt a little smug about scaring the daylights out of those two cats.) But as I was mentally patting myself on the back for being a good dad, I thought about how good God is and stopped congratulating myself.

God reminded me of Matthew 7 verse 11 *KJV* "If you, then, though you are evil, know how to give good gifts to your children, how much more will your Father in heaven give good gifts to those who ask him!"

I was able to be there for my son on that occasion but there have been times when I couldn't be there. There are and were many moments in the lives of my children when I can't or couldn't help them. At times I'm not even in the same state or same country. I felt good that Matty called for me and I responded... but I'm nothing as a father compared to Abba Father.

I want to remind you that the father in heaven wants a close relationship with you. He's waiting to hear from you. He's a loving father, not a boss, not a judge, and not a flawed man. There are never moments when we, his children, cry out to him and He won't be able to respond. He doesn't take vacations. He doesn't get distracted. Nothing can hinder Abba Father from having an amazing personal relationship with you, except you.

## CHAPTER 6
# IF YOU ONLY KNEW

### "If you only knew..."

That's what Jesus said in the book of John, chapter 4. No need to open your Bible or your Bible App, I got you, just read on.

If you're saved, you know the story of Jesus and the Samaritan woman at the well. You hear it preached and taught probably 4 times a year. In fact, you might have taught it or preached on it yourself. After all, there are so many points to glean from it.

If you're unfamiliar with it, I'll paraphrase it for you: Jesus was by himself, sitting on the edge of a well built long before. His disciples had gone to the city to buy meat. Jesus was tired, having traveled far, so he's sitting there when a woman came to draw water from the well.

Jesus asked her to draw water for him as well. The woman, a Samaritan, was surprised that he would even talk to her. Not because he was Jesus, the Christ – she didn't know that yet – but because Jews didn't deal with Samaritans. They were treated as second-class citizens. So this woman, who probably noticed a Jew sitting at the well she needed to draw water from, probably felt less than significant as she approached. Maybe she was expecting a sneer or for him to tell her to leave and come back after he had left. So, she was surprised that he even talked to her.

This isn't my main point but let me just say that people probably feel that way when you come around. A homeless person, an alcoholic, a drug-addict, an HIV patient, a felon – might feel inferior when you're in close proximity. How do you treat them? Do you cross the street? Do you ask for another

**Do you cross the street?**

table? Do you make sure to avoid eye contact? How do you treat these people that were fearfully and wonderfully made in the image of God?

Jesus spoke to the woman. He asked for water.

She replied, "How is that you, being a Jew, ask me, from Samaria, to get you a drink?"

Jesus replied, "If you only knew... "

I feel that God has said that to me on many occasions but mainly whenever I would worry about something. He might say the same thing to you whenever you're worried also. When God talks to me in those instances, it goes something like this, "If you only knew why you're going through this trial. I am

Alpha and Omega, I know the beginning and end of time and all that happens in between."

And time and time again, He comes through. Still, we worry about stuff, don't we? The reality is, it's hard not to worry when you're going through something. But we have to trust and understand that, in all things, He has a plan.

The same thing Jesus said to the woman, I want to share with you:

> If you only knew - you're going through communication and respect issues with your teenage son because He has a plan for other families who will go through the same and will need counsel. You are now part of that plan but in order to be their mentor, you have to go through it yourself.

> If you only knew - you're going through this state of depression so that you can lean on him like you used to. Your sister will be battling depression in a couple of years and your voice will be the only one that can reach her.

**If you only knew what God could do with the things He helps you through.**

If you only knew what God could do with the things He helps you through.

Jesus said to her, (John 4: 10 *KJV*) "If thou knewest the gift of God, and who it is that saith to thee, Give me to drink; thou wouldest have asked of him, and he would have given thee living water."

It's a great story. It ends with Jesus telling the woman things about her own life that no one but the Christ could know. She goes to the city and starts to evangelize. She tells everyone that would hear about the man named Jesus, who must be the Christ. Many people come to see him for themselves, and they come away saved.

I bring up this story because; stay with me here, that story didn't just happen when it happened. Allow me to explain myself. Something happened there long ago that created the atmosphere for those people to get to know Christ, many years later.

Jacob had dug that well many, many years before Jesus sat on it. The Bible refers to it as, Jacob's Well, but, although he dug it and it was once his, Jacob had given the land – and the well - to his son Joseph. Jacob must have benefitted from the well, but not fully. Not like Joseph who had the well in his younger years. And certainly not like Joseph's children who drank of the well since they were infants. Hundreds of years later, the Samaritan woman and many Samaritans would be blessed because of the well Jacob built. Not only from the water they drew from it, but because of that well, they were able to find living water.

If Jacob had not dug the well, there would never have been a place for the encounter to happen. When Jacob first broke ground, when he toiled under the sun, when he had to dig under rocks and vines, when he got dirty, sweaty, and then muddy, he had no idea how many people he was going to bless. He probably only dug it because he was thirsty. If he only knew...

Just like they were all blessed from the well, you and I are living off of the prayers that someone else prayed. We are benefitting from a foundation of the spreading of the gospel that we didn't lay. In other words, we are walking in a dimension of blessing that we didn't earn or deserve.

There will be prayers we offer up, that we sow, that we will reap. But there are seasons of our lives when, without us asking for it or working towards it, we will tap into new spiritual dimensions. Those blessing are for us in the same way that Jacob's life was enhanced by the well; it's for us, but not fully. It's more for those that will come after us.

John 4: 36-38 *NIV*, Jesus tells his disciples, "Even now the one who reaps draws a wage and harvests a crop for eternal life, so that the sower and the reaper may be glad together. Thus the saying 'One sows and another reaps' is true. I sent you to reap what you have not worked for. Others have done the hard work, and you have reaped the benefits of their labor."

Reaping is fun. We post it on social media when we reap, don't we? The new house, the new car, the new baby, the new suit, the promotion, and even the expensive dinner with the setting sun as a backdrop – we love to reap. And we should, especially if we toiled and sowed. But there's a difference in personal joy we should allow ourselves to feel, such as, if you were born in the ghetto and put yourself through school, got a great job, earned a promotion, and bought a new house, compared to if you were born with a silver spoon in your mouth and your parents bought you a house and you live there mortgage free. Wouldn't it be great to reap what you've never sown into?

I am personally reaping from prayers I've never prayed. I'm reaping from prayers and sacrifices that my father and his father before him made. The prayers they released to the heavens have come to fruition with me. Not just me but my siblings as well.

My father tells the story of when his mother heard her mother praying for her unborn children. His grandmother was praying for his mother's children, even though she wasn't married yet. So, before his father even met his mother, her mother was praying for him, my grandfather. She was digging a spiritual well for him that he could drink from many years later. She prayed that her daughter's children would walk in the ways of the Lord. Here I am, five generations removed from that prayer, serving the Lord and committed to serve the Kingdom of Heaven. By the grace of God, I am evidence of the seeds sown in prayer those many years ago.

If you live in the United States and you're not a Native American, you too are reaping from your ancestors. There was a moment in the history of your family that your forefathers came to this country, willingly or by force, but today, you are reaping from what they've sown.

One of the problems we as a nation face today is that we want everything instantly. It started decades ago with fast food, and then drive-thru's, and now, we can't stand to wait for anything, case in point, we even have an instant answer on a mortgage. We stop whatever we're doing when we get pinged on our phones, as if the text or post can't wait. It's as if the whole world is suffering from Attention Deficit Hyperactivity Disorder – ADHD. In the church, many people think God needs to speed up to match the times. Churchgoers know the principles of sowing and reaping but, for the most part, they think the process takes too long. In fact, many just want to reap! And those that sow aren't happy if they don't get credit for sowing!

If they only knew...

## New Coach

To call me a big fan of the game of basketball would be an understatement. I grew up playing ball with my brothers from sun up to sun down. We played every chance we got. When my son was born, I put a basketball in his crib. (I have the pictures to prove it!) Before he turned three years old I had already set up a little gym in the basement. At times he would lie on my chest doing bench presses. I started coaching him as soon as I felt he could handle it. I don't know if it's because he was born with it or because I started teach him at such an early age but by the age of 10, Matthew - aka "Matty" had a knack for the game.

As the years went by, we spent hours upon hours focusing on the game of basketball, either doing shooting drills, dribbling drills, watching games, or talking about it in the car. You could say it was "our thing." Many times, Matty would be the one to initiate the conversations. He genuinely developed a love for the game and enjoyed the challenge of competition.

It was no surprise that Matty developed into a young man with 'game.' One day, my younger brother Joey was with us and he took Matty to the side and started giving him some pointers. Matty was brought up to be a respectful young man, especially when it came to his uncles and aunts, but he paid a little special attention to Uncle Joey because Joey had played college basketball. I left them alone; happy Uncle Joey was imparting some wisdom on my son. When we got in the car, Matty was excited because he had learned so much.

As soon as we drove off he started, "Dad, Uncle Joey is a basketball genius. I mean, the way he sees the court, wow. One of the things he told me is that if a defender's lead leg is to the outside of my knee..." And he continued telling me what his uncle showed him; different moves, angles, creating space, and all sorts of good stuff. I was happy that Matty had learned all of that but not so happy that Joey was going to get the credit for all of it. I had been telling Matty that stuff for years!

I learned a spiritual lesson a few days later – one man sows and another man waters. Matty had heard it from me before but he needed a new voice. What mattered was that Matty had learned the lessons he needed to in order to get to the next level.

---
**One man sows and another man waters.**
---

I learned another spiritual lesson a few months later – you can't sow expecting credit. The goal in me teaching my son the game of basketball is for him to leverage his skills as best as he can so that his life can benefit from it, not for me to get any credit. If you're doing things for the kingdom to get the credit, your heart is in the wrong place. When your heart is aligned with God, you're not concerned with glory, you're concerned with revelation. People who care about their own status usually miss out on the revelation of what God really wants them to do.

I planted a seed in Matty that Joey watered. Since then, other coaches have also poured into him. When he gets to college, his coach there will benefit – will reap – from what collectively we have sown. The wins and losses won't go on our records but the coaches.

## It's not about you all the time

The true impact of the story of Paul and Silas is not that the Holy Spirit filled the place and their shackles dropped to the floor and they were set free. That's really cool stuff but that doesn't help anyone but Paul and Silas. The true impact of that particular story is that the jailor got saved! I would like to think that his family got saved. I would like to think that as a grandfather he taught his grandchildren about the Most High God.

In the same vein, the story about that Samaritan woman is not just about her. It's also about every single person that came from Samaria to meet Jesus who came away changed. But it's mainly about the well that was dug there years ago that created an atmosphere for miracles to happen. During the course of time from when Jacob dug it and Jesus sat on it, countless people were blessed by it. Long after the day God had ordained for Jesus to talk to the Samaritan woman, that well continued to bless others.

It's time to stop worrying so much about your ministry and how your words are immediately impacting those under the sound of your voice. You have to understand that true sowers sow without regard for who reaps or who gets the credit. True sowers don't sow for immediate benefit. True sowers sow for legacy, for generations.

# CHAPTER 7
# A WOMAN NAMED GRACE

## Biggest Impact To My Prayer Life

As I mentioned, Mona and I were only able to conceive one child. Yet, I am a father to five. When I met Mona, she had a daughter. A lively little girl named Tyveshe. She is who God used to shift my prayer life.

As what happens to millions of young people, Tyveshe began dabbling in drugs. It didn't take long for the drugs to take a hold of her and for her to live a "street life." Her dependency on drugs overrode every other facet of her life, including our family life. Tyveshe began to disappear for days on end, with us worrying sick about where she was, who she was with, what she was doing, why won't she come back home.

Many men I know who serve the Lord today credit a praying mother. A mother who kept praying for them even when everyone else figured, "well, he will never change". In Tyveshe's case, she had two praying parents. I never once accepted that our daughter would never know the joy of the Lord again. So I prayed and prayed and prayed for her. Countless times. I prayed with faith, I prayed through fear, I prayed with optimism, and I prayed with dread that she might not survive some nights.

> **I never once accepted that our daughter would never know the joy of the Lord again.**

I believe one of those types of prayers is what saved her on a particular instance. She had overdosed and had died. Yes, you read that correctly, she lay slumped over in a hallway of an apartment building. No one called 9-1-1 to save her life. There was a law that if someone were found with a person who overdosed, he or she would get arrested and charged being an accomplice. Miraculously, a police officer that knew us found her there and revived her.

Mona and I didn't know what to do. We had had sensible conversations with her, she had cried, we had cried, we had hugged and made promises to one another but shortly after she would be back on the streets. We tried to hold on to hope as much as possible but the reality of the situation was that Tyveshe was sinking deeper and deeper into a destructive lifestyle with no apparent help in sight.

There were many nights when the anxiety became more than I could handle and I would leave the house all hours of the night and go to the seediest sections in Brockton to look for her. When I would find her she would look at me in bewilderment, "I can't believe you found me!"

I would take her to a facility with promises being made that she was ready to change but those promises weren't as strong as the drug and pull of the streets. I had faith that God was about to do something but year after year passed without a hint of change.

During this time I went on a trip to Jerusalem with other Pastors. I met a man there called Adam Durso. We got along right off the bat and I confided in him the fear I had that one day we would get the news that she was dead. He looked at me somberly and told me about a New Life for Women program close enough to where we lived.

"Matt," he said, "if your daughter can get there, it will save her life."

Those words clung to my heart and I dared to breathe more hope into a seemingly hopeless situation. I had already taken Tyveshe to several programs/facilities but something struck my spirit when he said that. After talking to Mona about it, our prayers for our daughter no longer became the only course of action we took. We immediately began to pray for the program and sow financial seed into it. *If she can get there, it will save her life.*

"Lord," we prayed, "help us get her there."

Tyveshe found herself in trouble with the law, again, and her lawyer told us to expect her to get sentenced up to two years. I didn't know if that was a good thing or a bad thing. Maybe she needed a time-out for a couple of years to get her away from the influences around her. But then again, no parent wants their children to spend time in jail where there are even worst influences and atmospheres. Instead of the judge sentencing her to two years, he gave her to our custody! Finally, things were starting to change.

As soon as we got into the the car I told her I was taking her to New Life for Women, the place Adam Durso told me to take her. It was located in New Hampshire, a few hours drive away. I remember looking at Tyveshe suffering from withdrawals. She was a physical wreck. She wanted to jump out of the car and end her life, such was her misery. I began to pray in the spirit. Tears rolled down my face as I implored for God to show up in a mighty way. We needed a miracle and we needed it at that moment. We had prayed too much, we had suffered too much, she had suffered too much, we needed God the Father to step in.

## Grace

I called the facility, hoping they had room for her.

An angelic voice answered, "Hello, this is Grace, how can I help you?"

I told Grace our situation and that I was already on my way. I didn't know if they had room but I had faith to move mountains.

"It's okay Mr. Thompson, *just get her here...* "

I can't write well enough to explain how I felt when we got there except to say that when I walked through the doors to that facility I felt the very presence of Jesus. In my spirit I knew that chains had been broken there; generational chains, chains of alcoholism, chains of drug addiction, chains of pride, chains of ego, and every other chain that binds people.

They told me that it was a 4-day process to admit her to the facility. I told them we would do whatever it took, that I would stay there in New Hampshire until they could sort everything out. Then, the woman named Grace told me that she would be able to expedite the process. It was as if God's hand in our situation became visible.

When I left there, with Tyveshe securely admitted to the program, I made one simple prayer, "Lord, please anchor her here."

Although I am telling this story, I only played a part in it, it's Tyveshe's testimony to share. She was the one who had to fight off her demons and cravings. There were times when she would get up, pack up, and head to the front door. But to hear her explain it she says it was as if cinder blocks encased her feet and she couldn't move.

She stayed the course, glory to God. I pray that Tyveshe uses the testimony of her life for her to minister to others. I have no doubt that she is an agent of change for many women. I can't wait to see where God takes her.

## Faith Transactions

Life is constructed by a series of transactions. When most people think of a transaction they think something financial like a bank deposit or withdrawal. But there are transactions that happen all the time. Every conversation is a transaction of information. When you like a picture on social media there is a transaction. Every smile or frown is a transaction. What you put in your body is transaction. The lives that we live are the way they are because of the many small and big transactions we go through.

It's the same in the spiritual as it is in the natural. Faith transactions happen all the time. When the father of the demon-possessed boy brought him to Jesus and asked, "Can you do anything for him?" It was the beginning of a faith transaction.

Jesus asked him if he believed. The man said yes, but then added, "Help me overcome my unbelief."

I think that there are many people in God's Kingdom whose faith is like that mans. He believed yet needed help to overcome his unbelief. You have to understand that the man probably started with unwavering faith. He had brought his son to Jesus' disciples and they had made prayers and attempted to get the demons to leave the boy but they couldn't. So, in a sense, God had not answered the first time. Yet, he didn't give up. He went from the disciples to the master.

The man's son had been suffering since childhood. It could have been enough for the man to accept that his son was always going to be that way, especially after the disciples failed in liberating him. There might be moments, situations, and people in your life that have been the same way for many years. And it doesn't seem likely that things can change. But I'm here to remind you that the devil is a liar. Cry out to God an ask him to help you overcome your unbelief. Some faith transactions take longer than others. Some take mere seconds while others take a lifetime.

> **I'm here to remind you that the devil is a liar.**

Jesus healed the man's son because the man, although he struggled, proved by his actions of bringing the boy to him, that he had enough faith to provoke a transaction.

On another occasion, Jesus was walking in the middle of a multitude and someone touched him. Jesus looked around and asked, "Who just touched me?" He knew that a faith transaction had just transpired. The woman was healed without Jesus' active participation. He was just walking as the Son of God and a woman's life was changed.

There's a transaction on earth that is released in heaven. Faith powers it but consistency fuels it.

We all have a mountain that needs to be moved. Many times it's God himself who imparts a burden on us on who to pray for and, unwittingly, we become key cogs in whether or not the faith transaction happens or not. Oh, if you just had a faith the size of a mustard seed. Oh, if you just trusted in the power of your prayers. I declare that mountains will run from the sound of your footsteps in the spiritual realm.

## Grand – Fatherhood

Tyveshe has caused me to believe in God in a dimension of faith I would never had gotten to if not her. As a pastor it's easy to tell people to keep praying through their situations. We say it so often that it's almost an automatic response. But when you actually go through those 12 round heavyweight championship fights, when you've gone through spiritual warfare that kills the weak and scatters the timid, when you've exhausted all your tears and yet your body finds a way to produce more, to then see God show up – shifts your perception of how great the Great I Am really is.

I'd be remiss if I didn't also mention the blessing Tyveshe has been to me personally. After Mona gave birth to Matty, we figured we had cracked the code and would continue to have children. Nothing happened. No miracle follicles. No prophetic words. God had a different plan.

Tyveshe had her first daughter when Matty was two. She then had two more children. During the time she was afflicted by drugs, the department of Children and Families (DCF) entered the equation. They decided that her children would be better off as wards of the state. Her children, my grandchildren, were eleven, six, and six months old. Mona and I stood in the gap for our grandchildren and the state gave them to our custody.

I remember praying with all my heart and soul for God to allow Mona to be pregnant one more time. I gave God compelling reasons why to give us more children, I promised Him we would train them up in His ways and offer them to Him. After some of our prayers we were sure that God would see fit to open up Mona's womb again. But God, who knows all things, knew we were going to need the rooms to take in our grandchildren.

To say that we weren't able to give birth again is another lie of the devil. Mona and I have birthed many ministries for God's glory. We have birthed the message of hope, salvation, and love into many homes.

This very book, a project I had once given up on, is another child. A messenger dedicated to God to find you, wherever you are, and remind you that you are called for more.

What is your Amazing Grace Story? What is it that you're still in awe and grateful for?

_____

_____

_____

_____

Sometimes remembering the miracles God has done in our lives give us the faith for the miracles we are asking for Him now. What miracle are you believing God for right now?

_____

_____

_____

Why do you believe God can do it?

_____

_____

_____

**Personal Notes:**

_____

_____

_____

_____

_____

_____

_____

_____

_____

_____

_____

_____

_____

_____

_____

## CHAPTER 8
# A LIFE SENTENCE

## A time of turmoil

We are in the midst of an economic turmoil, not only us in the United States, but the world. New forms of global currency have begun to penetrate different soils. The racial divide in this country and around the world is as deep as ever. We are living in a time of wars and rumors of war; of "rogue" nations harnessing nuclear weapons. Individually, social media is attacking our senses like never before in the history of human kind. Also, and this one is by far the worst, there's a God-hating agenda disguised under innocent terms such as *tolerance* and *education* that is designed to kill the church of God. If there were ever a time to pray and cry out to God, it's now.

It's not a surprise when we fall, in fact, we fall often. But a good father is not necessarily concerned about the times you fall, He just wants to make sure you're able to get up again.

When my son was beginning to walk, he tripped and fell over and over again. At times he would start walking and his little legs would take him faster than he could handle. Mona and I would start chasing after him with outstretched arms but the little guy, with his little arms flailing all over to balance himself out, would fall over and over again. There were times when, after a good fall, he would cry loudly. So loudly in fact that I didn't think he would attempt to walk again for a while. But as soon as those tears were gone, he was up and on the go. I can't recall every time he fell but I can see in my head the times he got up and gave it another shot and another shot until he mastered it.

Regardless of what's going on in your life, regardless of how many times you've fallen, regardless of whatever wrong someone did to you, regardless of how many times you've been dropped, God is chasing after you with his arms outstretched. Pray to Him and he'll take your faults, sins, and transgressions and throw them into the sea. If you put your trust in Him, he'll give you a much better future than you ever thought you could live.

## 70 Years is a lifetime

There are many stories in the Bible that just blow my mind. I mean, its God's book so how can it not, right? But I want to bring up the story found in Jeremiah 29 in particular to help me make a point.

Everybody loves Jeremiah 29, verse 11 – "For I know the plans I have for you," declares the Lord, "plans to prosper you and not to harm you, plans to give you hope and a future."

It fills us Christians up with dreams of brighter days. People love that verse so much that by accident, many have memorized the following verses:

> Verse 12: Then you will call on me and come
> and pray to me, and I will listen to you.

> Verse 13: You will seek me and find me when
> you seek me with all your heart.

Very few verses in the bible warm our hearts like those. To know that God has a good plan for our futures is like knowing we are about to win a lottery. Like a good Snickers Bar, that verse satisfies. The reality is that those who were given that prophecy didn't get happy, not a bit. They didn't jump up and down in the spirit singing praises unto the Lord.

Those verses are a part of a letter the prophet Jeremiah sent to the surviving elders whom King Nebuchadnezzar had taken from Jerusalem to Babylon. The surviving elders... meaning, some of those who had been taken had already died or had been killed in captivity.

Jeremiah sends this letter and pretty much gives the rest of them a death sentence. First of all, God isn't happy with them.

In chapter 19 we see God say why he is going to destroy Babylon. He also states why them, the elders, are going to die too.

Verse 19: "For they have not listened to my words," declares the Lord, "words that I sent to them again and again by my servants the prophets. And you exiles have not listened either," declares the Lord.

What really gets me in this portion of the Bible though is that God tells them *when* he is going to deliver them. He tells them, through the letter, to build houses, to settle down, to plant crops, and even to allow their sons and daughters to marry.

God tells them, "When seventy years are completed, I will come to you and fulfill my good promise to bring you back to this place."

70 years! Remember, this letter is sent to the surviving elders! Basically, God is telling them to tell their kids to make a life in captivity because they are going to be there for a lifetime. He's telling the elders, make peace with your lives there because you are not coming back.

So, God is telling them to plant crops... for who? Not for them. God is telling them to seek peace and prosperity in the city...for what? Not for them. God is telling them to grow the settlement... why? Not for them. That's a tough word to digest. These elders are tasked to sow for something their eyes will never behold!

God is saying the same to you through this book. It's time to sow for something that's going to impact the next generation coming up behind you.

God told them to pray for the Babylonians. God is telling slaves to pray for their masters! To pray for those who have purposefully and irrevocably changed the very trajectory of their lives for the worst! Why would God ask them to do that?

I'll tell you why, because the next generation was going to reap from those prayers sowed!

When Jacob dug the well, it wasn't about him. It was about the generation behind him. When Jesus spoke to the Samaritan woman, it' wasn't about her, it was about the multitude that came to know Jesus. When the spirit of the Lord liberated Paul and Silas from jail, it wasn't about them, it was about the jailor, his family, and the other prisoners who were also freed. The common thread to these events is that someone had to first do something.

Dig a well. Plant a seed. Sow something that you don't expect to reap from. The next generation to emerge will come under an ungodly attack never before witnessed and they're going to need all the spiritual provisions this current generation can supply them.

You have been called for a time such as this. Humanity is crying for more children of God to stand up and speak life into deadly situations. God is looking for someone with the compassion and courage to speak things, not as they are, but as if they were. The moment you accepted God's love in your heart you have been given every spiritual gift. You may not know this but you are already equipped for God to send you into hostile environments with Good News.

I'll end with this...

There are places you will be called to go, things you have been designed to see, people you are destined to meet, and atmosphere's you have been equipped to change.

Child of God, you are an agent of change, a sower of life, and a digger of wells.

With God's favor and mercy, and with a mindset to bless others, go forth and shift the atmospheres.

# ACKNOWLEDGMENTS

Tyveshe, my daughter you are an inspiration and I am so blessed to be called your father. You are a miracle and a miracle worker.

Matthew Jr, my son, you are everything a father could hope for... greatness and generational transformation is yours.

Aaliyah, my granddaughter your tenacity and determination is amazing.

Jerome, my grandson you are a business man!

Peyton, my granddaughter you are My Chicken.

Dad, thank you for teaching me how to fight and cover my family in prayer "More is caught then taught."

Mom, I am beyond blessed to be loved by you. Our daily conversations mean more to me than you could ever know.

<u>To my incredible siblings:</u>
Andy, you are a genius

Theresa, you are a rock

Philip, you are the Maestro

April, you are a worship warrior

Joel, you are a pillar

Michael, you are a leader

Deborah, you are an angel

<u>Men of faith:</u>
Sumner, you are an amazing friend, brother and confidant

Zenzo, you are my prayer partner and friend

Adam, you have been a friend that is closer than a brother

Miles, you are a Big, Huge Deal

<u>My Team:</u>

Wil, you are an answer to prayer

Kym, you are a consistent warrior

Roberson, you are a visionary

Tamar, you are a conductor

Sophie, you are a driver

Aaron, you are 6 packs everywhere

Chris Bennett, you are a Godsend

Eli Gonzalez, my editor and new brother, thank you for your gift and your life of Faith

Peter Lopez, you are more than a publisher, you are family

Arch Bishop Garlington, Nana Barbara, Bishop McBath and Lady Janeen, Pastor David Ireland, Bishop Tudor Bismarck, Dr. Sam Chand, Dr. Sandy Kulkin, Prophet Gideon Danso, Pastor Edward Boateng, Bishop Timothy Clarke – Thank you, Thank you, Thank you, for the deposit of Faith and Motivation that you have given me.

And of course, to Jubilee... The Best Church in the World... we still have a lot of work to do and we're going to do it!

There are many more people to thank but I would forget some names. So I'll just say to everyone that has been a part of my journey or is walking with me just for this season, for all the prayers, well wishes, favors, times of laughter, friendships and fellowships, I thank God for you, dear Atmosphere Shifters.

# ENDORSEMENTS

## Atmosphere Book Recommendation

One of the joys afforded me is the opportunity to recommend books that have the potential to transform lives. This written account by Matthew Keith Thompson is one such book. Written from the valuable perspective of experience, the author shares insights from an obvious origin of revelation knowledge, an indication of divine encounter grounded in spiritual intimacy with God through the discipline of prayer and the pursuit of the path in the will of God for effective ministry. If your goal is to understand how a mature believer can yield to the lordship of Christ, obey the truth of God's Word, and move in the power of the Spirit for the purpose of creating an atmosphere that impacts the lives of those they touch, you should take the time to read this insightful account.

Bishop Dr. Gideon Andrew Thompson, DMin.
Founding Pastor Emeritus of Jubilee Christian Church,
Boston, MA
Senior Prelate of Church Without Wall, International

Headquarters: 1500 Blue Hill Ave., Boston, MA 02126

I have known Pastor Matthew Thompson for more than two decades. He is a most remarkable person who, with his talents could pick the arena in which he desired to be successful. Thankfully, for the Kingdom of God, for Jubilee Church, for the City of Boston, he chose the ministry. He's one of those rare mixtures of that combines an administrative gift and a creative gift. It finds expression in every area of his life. But most of all, he is a man of prayer – it is in his DNA, it affects the whole of who he is and the Church that he leads. Give these words your undivided attention; I promise you won't regret it.

Bishop Joseph L. Garlington, Sr
Presiding Bishop
Reconciliation! an International Network of Churches and Ministries

"Pastor Matthew Thompson is an eyewitness to an Atmosphere Shift of unprecedented reach in one of the most secular climates of our globe.

This book give insights into how to set the sails to capture the wind of the Spirit and navigate the waters of culture for maximum impact!

I highly recommend this book!!!"

Rev. Adam Durso, D.D.
Executive Director, LEAD.NYC

If you don't read this book, you would be missing out on one of the most powerful success principles. I don't know anyone who understands the "power of atmosphere" and how to use it for effective ministry and personal success more than Pastor Matthew K. Thompson.

Zenzo Matoga
Founder & Senior Pastor, Impact Church
Founder and director, UNOW.

# ABOUT THE AUTHOR

Matthew K Thompson was born to Bishop Gideon and Yvonne Thompson in 1972 in Boston Massachusetts, where he was also raised. He is the third of 8 children.

He is married to the love of his life for more than twenty-two years and counting, his Queen, Mona M. Thompson, and is a proud father to their two children, Tyveshe and Matthew Jr.

Since his youth, Pastor Matthew has exhibited a burning determination to advance the Kingdom of God. After graduating from Morehouse College in Atlanta, GA in 1996, where he had earned a basketball scholarship and played, his purposeful journey began. He has faithfully served as an Executive Assistant, Leader of Ministry of Helps, Executive Administration, Administrative Pastor, Executive Pastor, and now serves as the Senior Pastor of Jubilee Christian Church; a church with 7,000 members in multiple campuses.

"Pastor Matt" is uniquely called to help create order out of Chaos. His preaching style is dynamic and captivating, yet practical. His messages: Atmosphere Shift and Open Heaven, have captivated a generation.

Jubilee Christian Church, founded by his father, Bishop Gideon Thompson, has grown to be the largest church in the New England area. God has called Pastor Matt to preach all over the United States and to many foreign countries.

When not working for the Lord, Pastor Matt, an avid sports lover, loves to watch "Matty Jr." play basketball, and "his" New England Patriots. Rumor has it that when he laces them up, he still makes buckets.

Pastor Matthew K Thompson can be reached at PMKTministries@jubileeboston.com

CPSIA information can be obtained
at www.ICGtesting.com
Printed in the USA
BVHW04s0625200618
519457BV00002BA/11/P